Ch

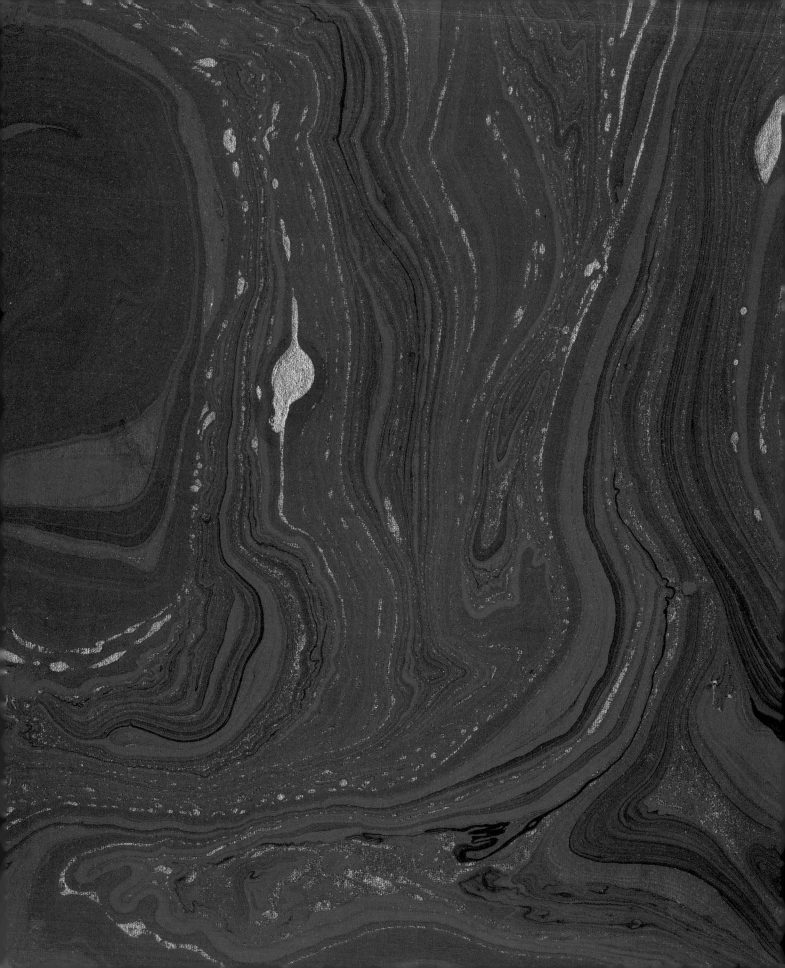

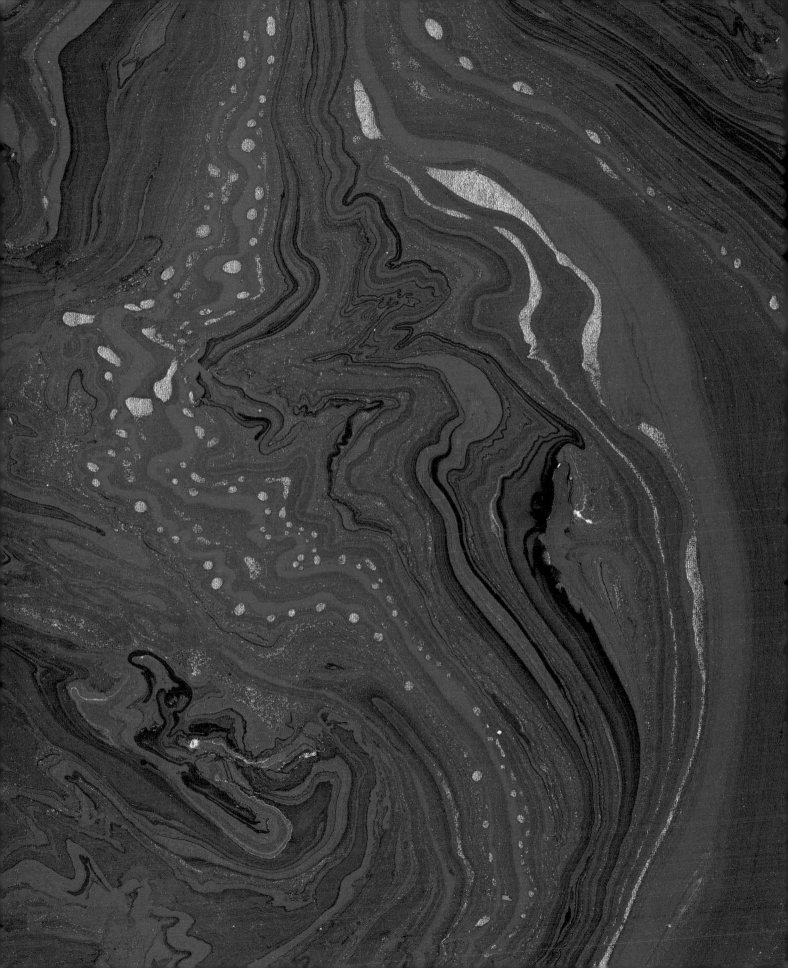

To Helen Randall — with much love **H.C.**

Text by Mary Joslin
Illustrations copyright © 2005 Helen Cann
This edition copyright © 2006 Lion Hudson

The moral rights of the author and illustrator
have been asserted

A Lion Children's Book
an imprint of
Lion Hudson plc
Mayfield House, 256 Banbury Road,
Oxford OX2 7DH, England
www.lionhudson.com

ISBN-13: 978-0-7459-4692-4 (hardback)
ISBN-10: 0-7459-4692-5 (hardback)
ISBN-13: 978-0-7459-6041-8 (paperback)
ISBN-10: 0-7459-6041-3 (paperback)

First hardback edition 2005
1 3 5 7 9 10 8 6 4 2 0
First paperback edition 2006
1 3 5 7 9 10 8 6 4 2 0

A catalogue record for this book is available
from the British Library

Typeset in 17/19 Venetian 301 BT
Printed and bound in Singapore

On that
Christmas Night

Mary Joslin

Illustrated by Helen Cann

LION
CHILDREN'S

The day was nearly over. The sun was slipping behind the hills, turning the green of the landscape to darkest grey.

'At least we have arrived in time to find a bed in Bethlehem,' said Joseph to Mary, as he tied the donkey beside the courtyard gate. 'Tomorrow we can find out how to register our names as Emperor Augustus requires.'

Joseph sighed as he went to find the owner of the place where he hoped to find lodging. It was hard, being one of the defeated nations in the Roman empire. You had to obey foreign laws, show respect for foreign soldiers, pay taxes to make others wealthy. For a moment, the mottled, red sky reminded Joseph of all the bloodshed and misery the Romans had brought.

Then the last rays of light faded, and all was dark.

'You want lodging?' The owner of the house looked concerned at Joseph's request. 'I'm sorry, but all my rooms are full. There are whole families crowded into some…'

'My wife is with me,' said Joseph desperately, 'and she's about to have a baby. Can you think of anywhere we could stay?'

As Joseph haggled and pleaded, other people gathered around.

'It's first come, first served,' reprimanded one. 'You've only yourselves to blame, arriving so late in the day.'

'Where I come from,' growled another traveller, 'no one is ever turned away. Does Bethlehem not offer decent hospitality?'

'Yes it does!' The owner's wife strode over indignantly. 'That young woman who's clearly expecting a baby has been left waiting outside for far too long. Of course we shall find a place. Where are the servants?'

She clapped her hands and began giving orders.

'Come,' she said to Joseph. 'Bring your wife with you. It will all be ready in no time.'

She led them to a low door at the far end of the courtyard.

'As you can see, this is really the animal room,' she explained, holding her lamp at arm's length so it shone into the shadows. 'But just give the servants a moment to clear it out a bit, and we can make it cosy and comfortable.'

She turned and smiled at Mary.

'It must be your first, you're only young,' she said kindly. 'Do you think it's a boy or a girl?'

'Oh, it's a boy,' said Mary confidently. She blushed and looked down.

Of course I'm sure it's going to be a boy, she thought. Nine months earlier, the angel Gabriel had come and spoken to her. 'God has chosen you to be the mother of a baby boy,' Gabriel had said. 'He will be known as the Son of God. God will make him a king, and his kingdom will never end.'

Mary and Joseph settled down in the straw. Their little donkey stomped and shuffled in the nearby stall. Beyond where he was tethered, an ox uttered a low bellow of contentment and munched noisily. Birds fluttered on the rafters – chickens, perhaps, or doves. It was hard to tell by the light of just one flickering oil lamp.

There, in the night, Mary's baby was born. She wrapped him snugly in swaddling bands as Joseph arranged straw and a blanket in a rough stone manger. Then she laid him down to sleep.

'Everything is just as the angel said,' Mary whispered to Joseph. 'Our baby is the one God has sent to save our people; and we are to call him Jesus.'

Out on the hills, some shepherds were keeping watch. In the low-walled fold behind them came the sound of their sheep, snuffling and shuffling. A night bird called in alarm, and a pack of ragged shadows darted among the bushes.

'Jackals,' said one shepherd to the others. 'Just let me see them when there's a bit more light. I'll have them with my slingshot.'

'Can't see much tonight,' replied one of his companions. 'There's no moon.'

'No,' said a third, 'but look at the stars. The sky is clear all the way to heaven. That's why it's so cold.'

As they looked, they saw a bright light. They all saw it. At first, it was as if a single star began to slide; then a cluster of stars began to move together, scattering sparkle in their wake. The sparkle swirled and rose up like an ocean wave... rising, cresting and tumbling in flakes of glittering gold.

In the midst of the light shone a face: kind and wise and ageless. And a voice spoke, deep and clear.

'Do not be afraid. I bring you good news, joy for all the world. This very night, in Bethlehem, a baby has been born: he is the one who will save your people, he is God's own son and king. This is how you will recognize him: he is wrapped in swaddling clothes and lying in a manger.'

Then the sky exploded with gold, swirling and dancing, and angel voices sang: 'Glory to God in heaven! Peace and goodwill to all!'

Then once again, all was silent; all was dark; all was shadow and mystery.

'Well,' said one shepherd, wide-eyed with wonder. 'What do you make of that?'

'Come on,' said another, pulling himself to his feet. 'We must go and see if any of this is true.'

They left their sheep and hurried up to Bethlehem. Joseph heard their footsteps in the street and waved the lamp to see who was passing by. In this way, the tiny light led the shepherds to Joseph and Mary and the baby. Everything was just as the angels had said.

What joy there was in the animal room as the shepherds told their story, and Mary knew more surely than ever that her baby was truly God's son.

Meanwhile, in lands far to the east, learned men had seen a star. 'The pattern in the heavens tells its message clearly,' they had agreed. 'A king has been born, in the land of the Jews. We must go and worship him.'

So they had set off, and the star had led them to the great city of Jerusalem, where they had made enquiries: Where was the newborn king? Had anyone heard news of him?

People shook their heads and eyed the strangers warily. There was already a king in Jerusalem, and his spies were everywhere.

Indeed, news of the travellers and their quest was soon taken to the palace where Herod the Great clung ruthlessly to power.

'I am king in Jerusalem,' snarled Herod to himself. 'It is none other than the emperor himself who has made me king. I have dealt with all my rivals. If there is any new threat to my power, I will deal with that also.'

He ordered the priests to be brought to him: 'Remind me of that prophecy in the scriptures,' he demanded, 'the one about a king, a Christ, God's chosen one. Where will he be born?'

'In Bethlehem,' they replied. 'It is written…'

Herod barely listened to their explanations. He wanted to see the travellers now, and he ordered that they come and visit him secretly, in the night. Once he had heard what they had to say, he knew they would believe the ancient prophecy. It became easy to persuade them to go to Bethlehem.

'Go there on my behalf,' he added slyly. 'When you find the king, let me know, and I too will make the journey to… pay my respects.'

As the travellers set off, the star shone above them, lighting their way. When it reached Bethlehem it hung quite still over the house where Joseph and Mary were taking care of their baby, Jesus.

'Truly, this must be the king,' the travellers agreed. They went inside and gave the baby rich gifts: gold, frankincense and myrrh.

In a dream, God's angel spoke to the travellers. 'Do not go back to Herod. That way means danger. Choose a different road home.'

In the same way, the angel spoke to Joseph: 'Take your family and hurry away to Egypt. King Herod means to harm the child.'

So, under cover of darkness, they all fled.

Only when it was safe did the little family return to their home in Nazareth. And each evening, as Joseph led his young son back from the day's work, Mary noticed how the starlight seemed to sparkle in Jesus' dark hair.

Then she remembered the promise of the angel, and the shepherds' story of a heavenly song, and the gifts offered by wise men by the light of a shining star.

She treasured in her heart all the wonder of that first Christmas night… the night when Jesus was born.

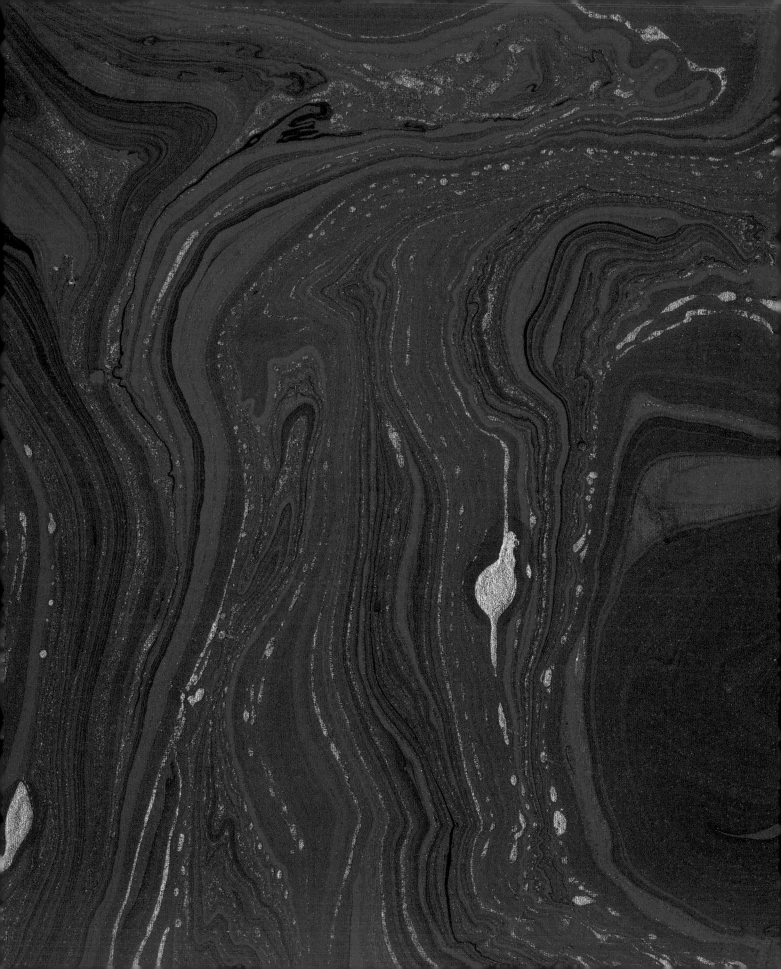

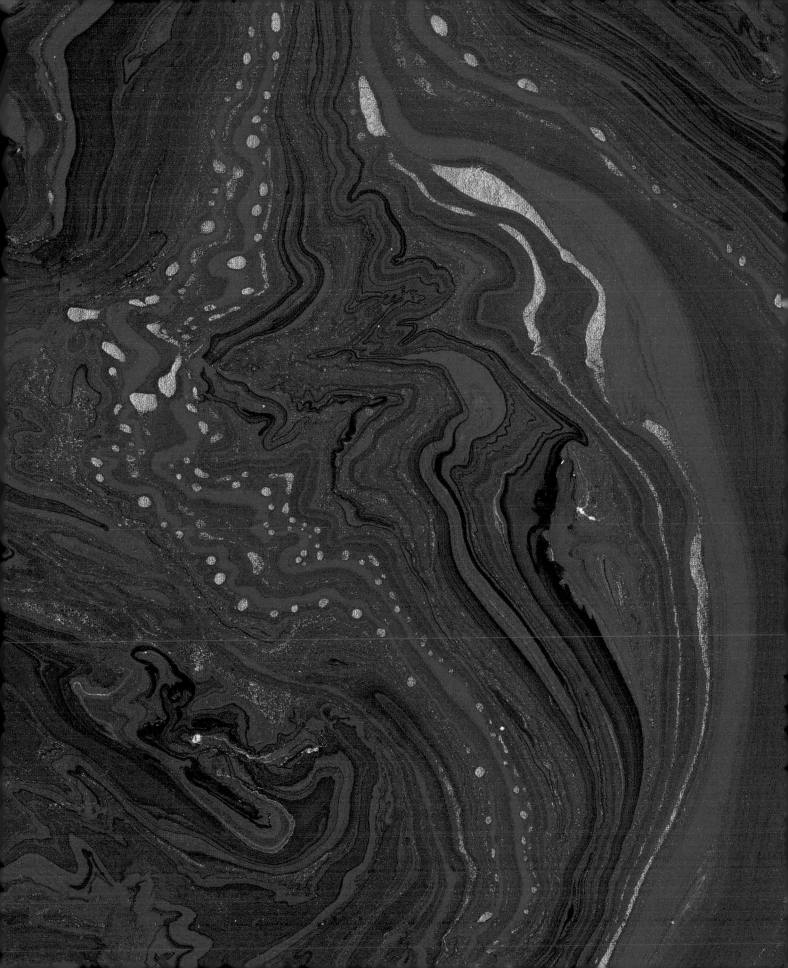

More Christmas books
from Lion Children's Books

Leah's Christmas Story
Margaret Bateson-Hill and Karin Littlewood

The Fourth Wise Man
Mary Joslin and Richard Johnson

Ituku's Christmas Journey
Elena Pasquali and Dubravka Kolanovic

Teddy Bear, Piglet, Christmas & Me
Catherine Maccabe and Clive Scruton

The Lion Storyteller Christmas Book
Bob Hartman and Susie Poole